8

THE WONDERFUL WORLD OF WORDS

The King Goes Dancing

Dr Lubna Alsagoff

PhD (Stanford)

Marshall Cavendish Children

Dancing is fun!

The king loved to dance.

The king loved to dance with Ari Article.

I'm Admiral Adjective.
I take care of adjectives.

The king loved to dance
with Admiral Adjective.

I'm Count Quantifier.
I take care of quantifiers.
Quantifiers tell you how many
of something there are.

The king loved to dance with Count Quantifier.

The king could dance by himself.

Noun

flowers

children

We can use nouns by themselves to describe things, people, animals and places.

We can use nouns by themselves in sentences.

_____ must be worn at all times!

_____ are so quiet you can hardly hear them coming.

You could give your mother _____ for her birthday!

_____ were allowed to enter the fun fair free of charge.

We must plant _____ to help WOW stay green and beautiful!

We need _____ to guard the castle.

King Noun could dance with his favourite page, Ari Article.

	Article		Noun
	a		bird
	the		
	a		
			egg
	the		
			clock

Articles help nouns to talk about things, people, animals and places.

We can use nouns together with the articles *a*, *an* or *the* in sentences.

_____ just flew into the room!

I will pack _____ in my bag.

You can sit under _____ to rest.

I like to eat _____ every day for breakfast.

_____ are beginning to bloom.

I need _____ in my room so I can tell the time!

He could dance with his best friend, Admiral Adjective.

Adjective	Noun
hungry	children
	flower
tall	
brave	
	shoes

Adjectives also help nouns to describe things, people, animals and places.

_____ have eaten all the food in the kitchen!

You can find _____ growing in the gardens of WOW.

_____ line the road leading to WOW Castle.

There are _____ sleeping in the basket

We need _____ to guard the castle.

_____ must be left at the door!

The king could dance
with Count Quantifier.

Quantifier   Noun

two

many

some

birds

_____ are still guarding the castle gate!

I saw _____ in the basket.

There are _____ in the garden.

The queen only has _____.

_____ have come to see the prince.

I can see _____ perching on that branch.

The king could dance with Count Quantifier and Admiral Adjective.

Q Quantifier	Adjective	N Noun
	playful	
	shiny	
	curious	

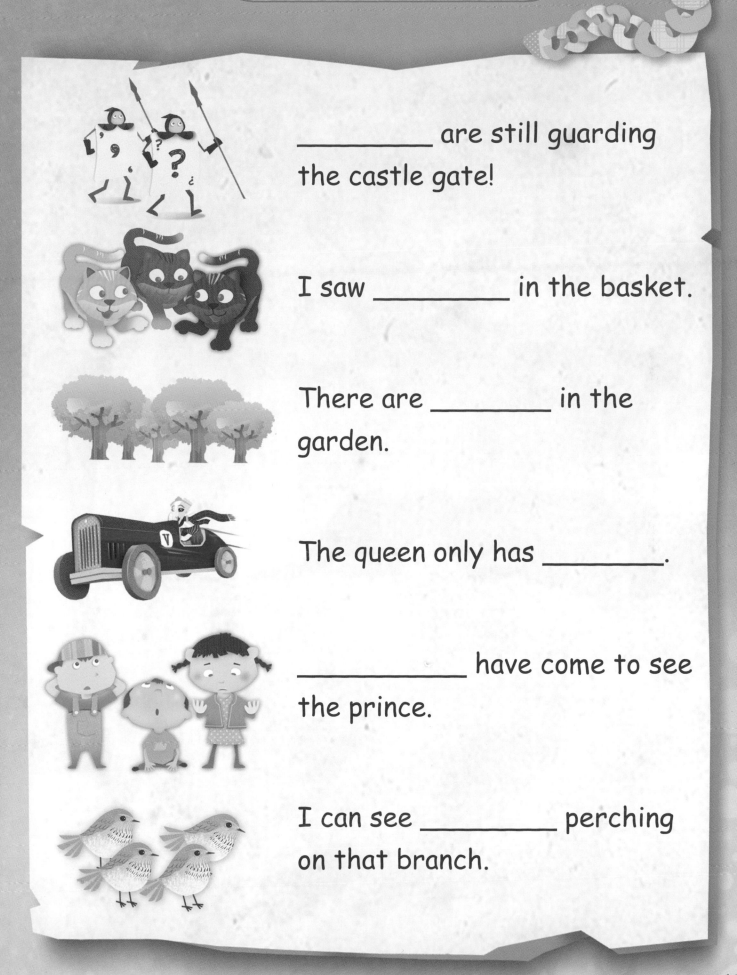

_____ are still guarding the castle gate!

I saw _____ in the basket.

There are _____ in the garden.

The queen only has _____.

_____ have come to see the prince.

I can see _____ perching on that branch.

13

The king could dance with Ari Article
and Count Quantifier.

The king could also dance with all the three of them.

Articles, quantifiers and adjectives tell us more about nouns. These words together with the noun make noun groups (also called noun phrases).

With just 4 words, we can make 8 different noun groups:

children, hungry, the, two

Article	Quantifier	Adjective	Noun
			children
		hungry	children
	two		children
the			children
	two	hungry	children
the		hungry	children
the	two		children
the	two	hungry	children

Draw your own table and try to make more noun phrases. Remember to use the words in the right order!

pencils, the, ten, sharp

foxes, fifty, the, hungry

bottles, the, six, green

The Fabulous Forest of WOW
This is a wonderful book!
We must thank Magpie for bringing it to us.
Yes, but where is Magpie?
THE WOW GRAMMAR BOOK

In a different part of the forest, Magpie is very happy. She loves all the shiny and beautiful things in her nest.

Use nouns to name the things in Magpie's nest.

r [ ] [ ] g

k [ ] [ ] [ ]

m [ ] r [ ] r

p [ ] [ ]

[ ] [ ] [ ] o n

But Magpie wasn't happy about one thing.

I wish I could find that lovely shiny shoe.

Now this was the last place I saw the shoe.

So Magpie decided to look for the shoe.

Magpie looked everywhere.

Suddenly, she saw a
strange and enormous giant!

It was Princess Preposition. She had come to look for her father's shoe.

Magpie realised who the stranger was!

Are you the princess from the kingdom of WOW?

Magpie was very excited
to see the princess.

Dear Parents,

In this issue, children should notice and learn:

- Nouns can combine with many different words to describe something or someone.
    - with an article, a/the
    - with quantifiers — words that tell you how many, e.g., one, two, three, many, few, some
    - with adjectives

- There are many ways that nouns can combine with these words. Nouns can sometimes combine with all of them, or one or two of them, or none at all.

- But in all the combinations of a noun group/phrase, the different words that combine with the noun must be in the right order: Article + Quantifier + Adjective + Noun

- The noun is the head of the noun group/phrase, so it must always be present.

Page	Possible Answers
4-5	shoes | kittens | flowers | children | trees | soldiers
6-7	a bird | the shoes | a tree | an egg | the flowers | a clock
8-9	hungry children | beautiful/wild/colourful flowers | tall trees | cute/cuddly kittens | brave soldiers | dirty/muddy shoes
10-11	two soldiers | three kittens | many trees | one car | some children | four birds
12-13	two brave soldiers | three playful kittens | many tall trees | one shiny car | some curious children | four blue birds
15	pencils | the pencils | ten pencils | sharp pencils | the sharp pencils | the ten pencils | ten sharp pencils | the ten sharp pencils
17	ring | key | mirror | pen | spoon